MUD TO THE RESCUE!

How Animals Use Mud to Thrive and Survive

TANYA KONERMAN   ILLUSTRATED BY MELANIE CATALDO

Web of Life
CHILDREN'S BOOKS

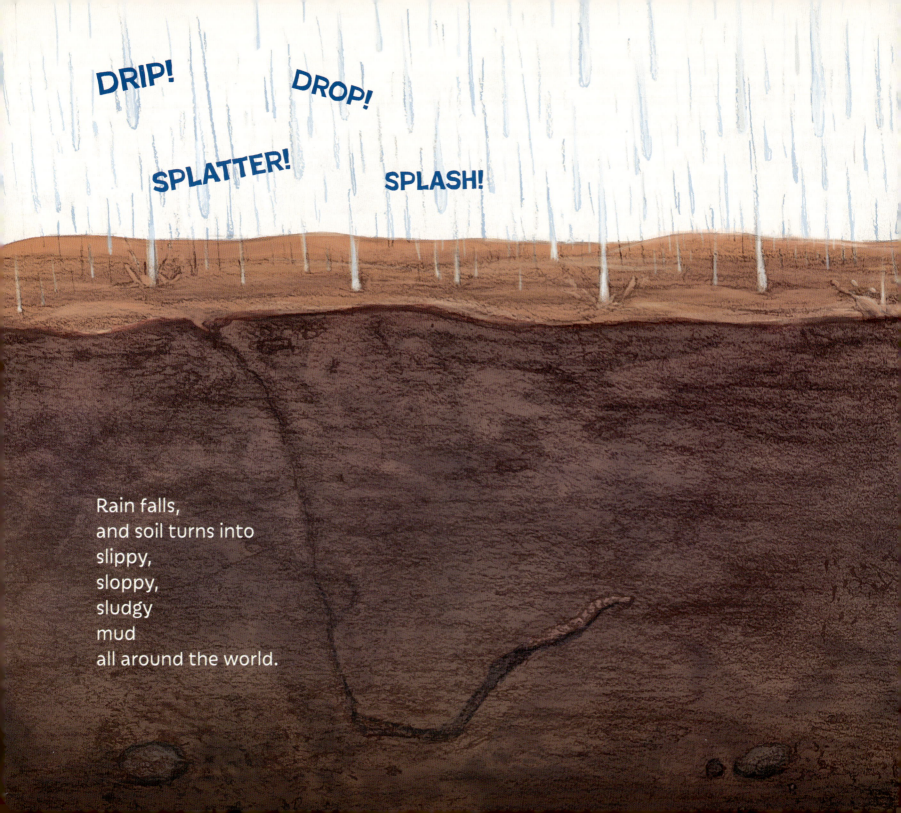

DRIP! DROP!
SPLATTER! SPLASH!

Rain falls,
and soil turns into
slippy,
sloppy,
sludgy
mud
all around the world.

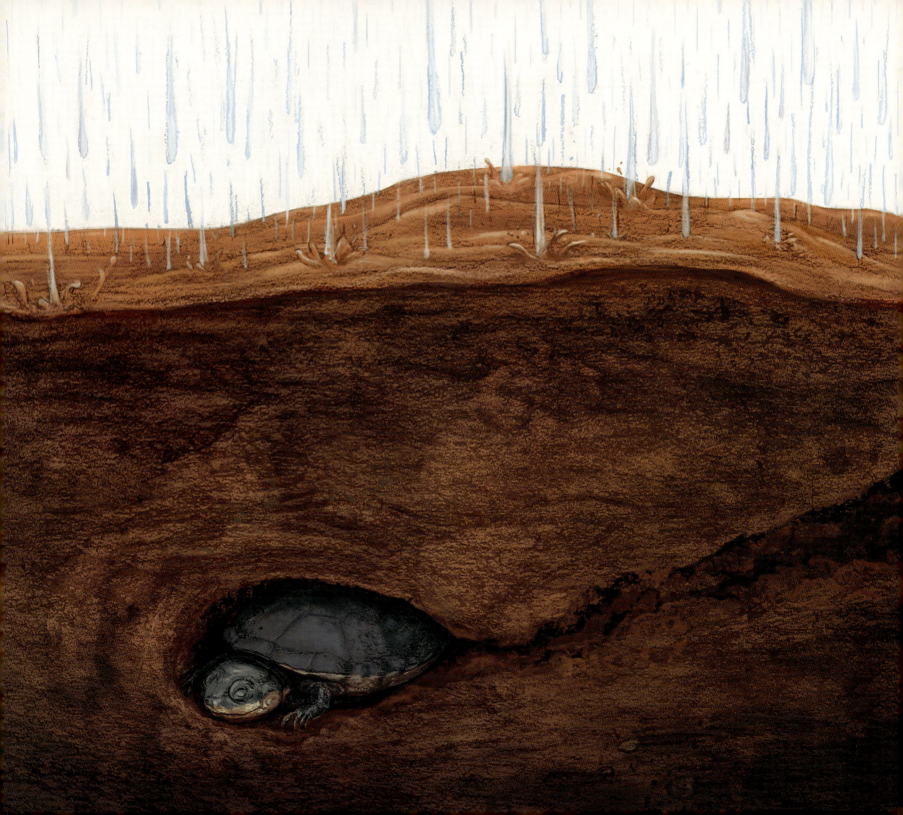

In open grasslands,
the sun swelters,
scorches,
sizzles,
shimmers.

African Elephant can't sweat
and doesn't have enough hair
to block burning rays.

Hippo has skin that *craaaacks* when it's dusty and dry.

MUD...

...to the rescue!

Wallowing in squishy mud baths cools, comforts...
Aaaaah!

Biting bugs are bothersome... ouch!

*A nice layer of mud blocks pests and **parasites** that itch or make elephants and hippos sick.*

Among the leaves,
birds are busy.
Helmeted Hornbill and Magpie-lark
need strong materials
to hold together their homes.

MUD...

...to the rescue!

A little potty talk...

The female helmeted hornbill disposes of feces (that's poo) through the mud wall's tiny crack. This keeps her nest clean and keeps predators from smelling her and her chicks.

Male Helmeted Hornbill
carries soil in his beak to mix with...
saliva, poo, or wood.

Magpie-lark starts with
mud and adds...
twigs, feathers, and grass.
Nests cozy and safe inside and outside!

Through frigid, frozen winters, Painted Turtle can't endure the icy, cold climate.

While in harsh, harmful heat, African Helmeted Turtle can't survive the long desert droughts.

MUD...

...to the rescue!

Beds of deep, squashy mud offer just the trick to protect their bodies during **hibernation** or **estivation**.

"Hello... What year is it?"

African helmeted turtles bury themselves in the sludgy bottom of watering holes and stay inactive in this cool dampness for months— or even years!

Below the moonlight,
Duck-billed Platypus swims.
As the tide goes out,
Mud Crab climbs ashore.
Both are hungry.

This may shock you...

Duck-billed platypus has a rubbery snout that can sense its prey's tiny **electrical currents** in the mud.

MUD...

...to the rescue!

Duck-billed Platypus
finds delicious
worms, frogs, and insects
in the squelchy mud.

MMMM!

While scurry, scurry...
Mud Crab feasts on
bivalves, barnacles, snails,
and even—watch out!—other crabs.

CRUNCH!

Near the water,
it's time to start a family.

Flamingo lays one egg, and American Alligator lays up to seventy. Wow! They both need to protect their unhatched young.

MUD...

...to the rescue!

Flamingo parents make a tower of sturdy mud with their beaks and feet.

If we only had a shovel...

Because the flamingos are building upward, it can take a pair up to six weeks to finish their mud nest!

American Alligator builds an above-ground mansion to house eggs and control the eggs' temperature.

Under glittering, glimmering, sparkling, shimmering stars, Pond Beaver and River Otter want to make hideaway homes with swim-up doors.

...to the rescue!

Pond Beaver spreads mud and grass around a frame to build a secure dome-shaped lodge.

Talk about busy beavers!

A pond beaver's lodge can be as tall and wide as a school bus!

Berries burst,
seeds split,
guava gushes.

But eating tasty treats
in big batches is dangerous
for Amazon Fruit Bat
and Green-winged Macaw.

MUD...

...to the rescue!

To counter poisons and
calm upset stomachs,
or add minerals to their diets,
they eat mud—
it soothes and sustains!

Pass the mud, please!

Eating mud to help the body is called **geophagia**, and it is recorded in over 200 species of animals. Even humans used mud this way in the past.

Worth waking up for?

Given enough space, pigs may enjoy a morning mud wallow of up to three hours!

Many creatures—
crafty, cunning, clever—
find mud helpful.
But for some, it's also...

More About Mud-lovers:

African Elephant: Many African elephants live in very hot and dry climates on the savannas in eastern and southern Africa. Because their dark skin absorbs the sun's burning ultraviolet (UV) rays, they need a sunblock—MUD. A layer of wet, thick mud also helps them to stay cool since they're unable to sweat.

Hippopotamus: Hippos have a very thin outer layer of skin that dries out easily in the hot African sun. So, hippos spend most of their time in water and mud to keep their skin moist and to fight dehydration. They also secrete an oily, thick reddish substance called "blood sweat," which acts as a sun barrier. It blocks UV rays from the sun and helps prevent infections in the hippo's skin.

Helmeted Hornbill: Helmeted hornbills mate for life. At nesting time, a pair works together to seal the female inside a tree hollow. They use the sides of their long bills to press mud into an almost solid wall. For three to five months, the male passes food to the female (and later, their chicks)—figs, fruits, squirrels, and even snakes—all through a half-inch (1.3-centimeter) crack. (Food too large is eaten first then regurgitated.) Eventually, the female breaks out of the nest, then she helps rebuild the mud wall and feed her chicks until they are also ready to break out.

Magpie-lark: This bird is also known as the peewee because of its unusual call. To build a nest, the male and female gather wet mud in their beaks. They form a bowl-shaped nest, both on and around a straight branch set unusually high in a tree—up to sixty feet (18 meters). (That's higher than a tower of four female giraffes standing one on top of another!) Then the peewees line their nests with feathers, fur, grass, and sticks for warmth and allow the mud to mix in to make it stronger.

Painted Turtle: This turtle lives in shallow ponds, creeks, lakes, and marshes. In winter, it cannot manage its energy levels or muscle activity because temperatures are too cold. So, it buries itself in mud up to three feet (about 1 meter) deep under the water or on shore. It enters **brumation**—a form of hibernation for cold-blooded animals—for up to six months. In order to survive under water and mud for this long, it takes in oxygen from the water through special blood vessels in its rear end!

African Helmeted Turtle: This turtle lives in streams, ponds, and marshes. It eats plants, clams, insects, fish, birds, small reptiles, and even dead animals (yuck!). During dry weather, the African helmeted turtle estivates in mud. It can live on water and nutrients stored in its body while its body's systems are slowed down.

Duck-billed Platypus: The duck-billed platypus does not have teeth. So, first, it uses thousands of tiny receptors in its flat snout to feel the electrical currents emitted by the muscles of its prey. Then the platypus scoops food, mud, and gravel from the river or lake bed and stores them in its cheek pouches. When it surfaces, it mashes everything together, using the mud and gravel like teeth to break up the food.

Mud Crab: Mud crabs—also called muddies—live in coastal wetlands. They stay in mud burrows during the day and come out to eat at night. Their eyes are set on top of their heads like periscopes and help them spot food and see in a full circle! They also have tiny hairs on their leg tips for touch and taste. Strong, powerful claws allow them to eat underwater prey with shells, including other crabs.

Flamingo: Flamingos live in mudflats and lagoons, or on shallow lakes. A male and female work together to build a nest by using their beaks to push mud toward their feet until a tall mound is formed. They often add straw, feathers, sticks, and stones. Then they shape the top like a bowl to hold a single large white egg. The nest may be one to two feet (0.3–0.6 meters) tall to protect the egg from rising water and heat near the ground.

American Alligator: The American alligator builds a nest of grass and mud above ground. This nest is three and a half to six feet (1 to almost 2 meters) across and one to two feet (0.3–0.6 meters) high. The female lays twenty to seventy eggs. The temperature of the nest while the eggs incubate determines the sex of the hatchlings: 90–93°F (32.2–33.9°C) makes males, 82–86°F (27.8–30.0°C) makes females. Temperatures between those make a mix of males and females.

Pond Beaver: At night, beavers make a new home called a lodge using their powerful front paws to scoop mud from the pond's bottom or banks. They chew branches or tree trunks to create a framework and pat mud in between to finish a mound. This super-strong wall keeps out both water and predators like foxes and wolves.

River Otter: River otters often live near beaver lodges. They dig burrows into the banks of a river, pond, or marsh. These tunnels start above or below the water and lead into the muddy bank where they make a dry nesting chamber called a den. Here, the females give birth to three or four pups each spring. River otters can grow to four feet (1.2 meters) long and up to twenty-five pounds (11 kilograms)!

Amazon Fruit Bat: The Amazon fruit bat sometimes eats unripe fruits, leaves, and seeds that contain toxins, which upset its gut. To counteract the poisons, it visits a clay lick. (Clay is a component of mud.) The bat eats the clay, which binds with the toxins and helps them leave its body faster.

Green-winged Macaw: This three-foot-tall (almost 1-meter-tall) "gentle giant" eats fruits, seeds, leaves, and nuts. Eating clay helps to remove toxins in these foods from its gut. See the Amazon fruit bat description above for more about how this works. This bird also eats clay to gain important minerals such as iron, sodium, calcium, and magnesium. These are vital for its energy and health.

Domestic Pigs: Pigs, like many other animals, use mud to prevent sunburns and to stay cool since they can't sweat. They also wallow to control parasites and to mark their territory. But there's another important reason why pigs and mud go together. Pigs wallow in mud as a natural behavior and enjoy it! Without the regular chance to do so, they can become stressed and unhealthy. A mud-covered pig is a happier pig.

People: Even people use mud. Around the world, mud is used to build houses and grow food. It's also applied to human skin to treat arthritis, back pain, acne, dandruff, and other ailments (or as beauty treatments)! Scientists are using mud to help save coastal tidelands from rising sea levels. And some people are even using it to create art. How do you use mud?

Glossary

bivalves – mollusks such as clams or oysters, which have a soft body, two shells that are hinged together, and gills

brumation – a way for a cold-blooded animal to conserve energy by being inactive during winter; unlike in hibernation, the animal may still seek water and/or food on warmer days

electrical currents – the flow of electricity through something, such as mud, water, or air

estivation – when an animal enters a sleep-like state during a hot or dry period, in order to conserve energy and reduce the need for food and water when those resources are limited

geophagia – eating soil, clay, chalk, or ground-up rock; this practice helps animals to gain needed minerals; protects the gut from toxins, bacteria, or corrosion; or helps treat diarrhea

hibernation – when an animal enters a deep resting state, with very slow breathing and heart rate, to protect it from cold in the winter; during this time, it can go without eating or drinking water by using its fat reserves to survive

parasites – animals that live in or on another animal that they get nourishment from and may harm in the process

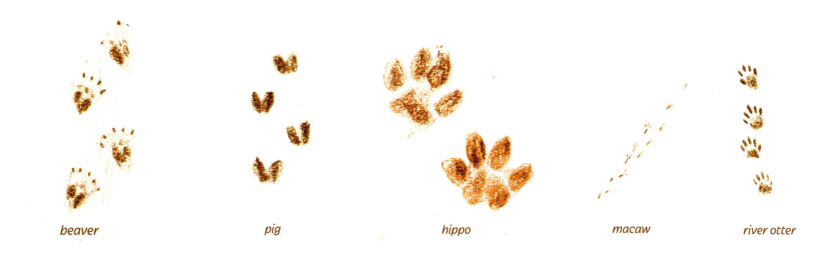

beaver *pig* *hippo* *macaw* *river otter*

Author's Note

When I first started thinking about animals who use mud, of course I thought about elephants and pigs. Then I started reading about other animals who also seek out mud, and who use it every day, and the list kept getting longer, and longer, and longer! It really is amazing how many creatures around the world use mud—perhaps hundreds!

I chose the animals in this book because they are pretty cool to read about. But I also chose them because they each use mud in a way that many other animals, insects, birds, fish, and other creatures use it as well. And scientists are smart, but there might be ways that animals use mud even they haven't figured out yet. Maybe if you keep your eyes open, you might discover a new and exciting way your favorite creature is using mud!

To Learn More

Eaton, Maxwell. *The Truth about Hippos*. Roaring Brook Press, 2018.

International Elephant Foundation Organization (website at: Elephantconservation.org).

Hanna, Jack. *Jack Hanna's Wild but True!: Amazing Animal Facts You Won't Believe!*: Media Lab, 2016.

Hirsch, Rebecca E. *Platypuses: Web-Footed Billed Mammals*. Lerner Publications, 2015.

National Geographic Kids Animal Encyclopedia 2nd Edition: 2,500 Animals With Photos, Maps, and More! National Geographic Kids, 2021.

Owen, Ruth. *Mud & How It Helps Animals*. Ruby Tuesday Books, 2021.

The David Sheldrick Wildlife Trust (website at: www.sheldrickwildlifetrust.org).

The National Parks Service (website at: www.nps.gov).

For my Mud Lovers: Mike, Abby, Seth, Krista, and Grace ~ T.K.
For Ramona and Dan with mud ♥ ~ M.C.

Text © 2025 by Tanya Konerman
Illustrations © 2025 by Melanie Cataldo

For ages 4-8

All rights reserved. No part of this book may be reproduced or utilized in any form or by any means, electronic or mechanical, including photocopying, recording, or any information storage in a retrieval system, without permission in writing from the publisher.

Library of Congress Control Number: 2024939416
ISBN: 978-1-970039-09-2

Book design by Marlo Garnsworthy, Icebird Studio, www.IcebirdStudio.com.
Published in the United States in 2025 by Web of Life Children's Books, Berkeley, California.

The artwork in this book was created using pencils, paper, and digital paint.

Printed in China by Toppan Leefung Printing.

For free, downloadable activities, and for more information about our books and the authors and artists who created them, visit our website: www.weboflifebooks.com.

Distributed by Publishers Group West/An Ingram Brand
(800)788-3123
www.pgw.com